PEARSON LANGUAGE CENTRAL for MATH

PEARSON

Glenview, Illinois • Boston, Massachusetts • Chandler, Arizona • Upper Saddle River, New Jersey

Language Central for Math
Fitchburg Public Schools Curriculum Project Team

Principal Author
Patricia Page Aube

Contributing Authors
Grades 6–8
Patricia McCormack
Amy Redder
Miriam Ruiz
Evelyn Santana
Sean Walker
Lindsey DiMauro Wheeler

Project Director
Bonnie Baer-Simahk

Technical Assistance
Richard Lavers

Sponsor
Massachusetts Department of Elementary
and Secondary Education's (ESE) Office
of English Language Acquisition, 2009.

Cover Art: Lorena Alvarez

ISBN-13: 978-0-13-253764-3
ISBN-10: 0-13-253764-8

2 3 4 5 6 7 8 9 10 V064 14 13 12 11 10

How to Use Language Central for Math

This book will help you **think, talk,** and **write** about what you are learning in your math class. Every lesson has 4 pages to help you learn the language needed to succeed in math.

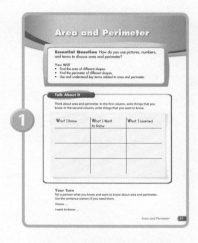

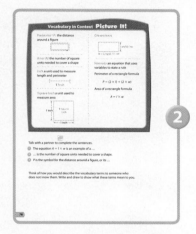

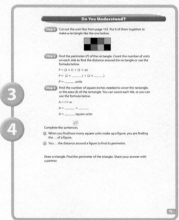

1. Activities connect what you know with what you will learn.
   Look for the **blue box** on the first page.

2. Vocabulary terms are shown with pictures to help you learn what they mean.
   Look for the **red box** on the second page.

3. Look for clues to help you know when to write an answer ✏️ and when to speak an answer 💬 .

4. Practice the skills you learn in your math class.

CONTENTS

Addition Story Problems

Essential Question What terms do you need to use to explain how to add integers and solve problems?

You Will
- Identify the operation needed to solve problems.
- Solve story problems with addition of integers.
- Use vocabulary terms to explain how to solve problems.

Talk About It

Rate the following mathematical terms according to the following scale:

1 I have never heard this term before.

2 I have heard this term before, but I don't know how to use it in mathematics.

3 I understand the meaning of this term and know how to use it in mathematics.

_____ Addition/Add	_____ Integers
_____ Calculate	_____ Expression
_____ Positive Value	_____ Total
_____ Zero	_____ Negative Value
_____ Represent	_____ Rational Numbers

Your Turn

Work in pairs or small groups. For each term that you rated a 2, complete these sentence starters.

I have heard the term …

I think it means …

Vocabulary in Context **Picture It!**

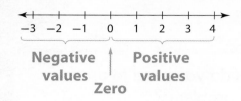

Negative values | **Zero** | **Positive values**

Integers Set of positive whole numbers, their opposites, and zero

$$-5, -1, 0, +3, +998$$

Rational Numbers Include integers, fractions, and decimals

$$1, 0, -5, \frac{1}{2}, -\frac{2}{5}, 0.4, -0.002$$

Addition/Add

$$\begin{array}{r} 234 \\ +345 \\ \hline \end{array}$$

Total or **Sum** ⟶ 579

Represent Stand for; be a symbol of

Expression Numbers, symbols, and/or operation signs grouped together. An expression may have a **variable.**

$$2 + 4 \qquad n + 523$$

Calculate To find an answer

Talk About It

Work in pairs or small groups. Use the sentence starters and the vocabulary terms to talk about the story problem below.

There are 2 cups of water in a pan. Bill puts 3 more cups of water in the pan. What is the total amount of water in the pan?

1. To solve this problem you need to find …

2. The operation you will use to solve this problem is …

3. You can write 2 + 3 to solve this problem. 2 + 3 is an …

Your Turn

A notebook costs $5. A pen costs $2. What is the total cost if you buy a notebook and a pen?

To solve the problem, use the operation of … to … the …
The … used to solve the problem is 5 + 2.

You can use two-color counters to add integers. The red side represents positive values. The yellow side represents negative values.

+1
positive value

−1
negative value

If you have 1 positive-value counter and 1 negative-value counter, you have a zero pair. The zero pair shows that $+1 + (-1) = 0$.

zero pair: ● + ○ = 0

Use two-color counters to find $+3 + (-5)$.
    Show 3 red and 5 yellow counters.

    Make as many zero pairs as you can.
    There are 3 zero pairs.

    2 yellow counters are left unpaired.
    So, $3 + (-5) = -2$.

Talk About It

Work in small groups. Use the vocabulary terms and sentence starters as you solve this problem.

Joanna got $+1$ point for every word she spelled correctly. She got -1 point for every word she spelled incorrectly. She spelled 6 words correctly. She spelled 2 words incorrectly. What was her total score?

1 To solve the problem, you need to …

2 Use two-color counters to add $+6 + -2$. Make as many zero pairs as you can. After you make zero pairs, there are … counters left.

3 Find the answer to the problem. Joanna's total score, is …

Your Turn

Work in pairs. Create your own addition story problem. Share it with your partner. Use the vocabulary terms and sentence starters from the lesson to talk about the problems you created.

Think, Talk, and Write

Your Turn

When you solve a story problem, think about these steps.

- Understand the words in the story problem.
- Know what question is being asked.
- Decide what operation to use and write an expression.
- Find the value of the expression. Use two-color counters to help.
- Give the answer to the problem.

In two rounds of a game, Josh scored -5 and $+9$.
What was his total score after those two rounds?

Work in pairs. Discuss each step you use to solve this problem.
Then solve the problem.

Talk and Write About It

Use the sentence starters to help you solve this problem.

Angelina had 12 apples in a basket. She put 6 more apples in the basket.
What is the total number of apples in Angelina's basket?

1. I am asked to find _____.

2. The operation I will use will be _____. The expression
   I will use is _____.

3. The value of the expression is _____.

4. The answer to the problem is _____.

Produce Language

Paula scored -5 points in round 1. In round 2 her score was 4 points higher
than in round 1. What was Paula's score in round 2?

Use the steps above. Write how you solved the problem. If you used
two-color counters, draw a picture or write about how you used them.

Operations

Essential Question What terms and symbols do you need to know and use to learn about operations in mathematics?

You Will
- Learn which symbols go with which operations.
- Understand how to use mathematical symbols.
- Use the correct vocabulary when talking about operations and their symbols.

Talk About It

Rate these mathematical terms according to the following scale:

1. I have never heard of this term before.

2. I have heard this term before, but I do not know how to use it in mathematics.

3. I understand the meaning of this term and know how to use it in mathematics.

_____ Scientific Notation		_____ Multiply/Multiplication
_____ Subtract/Subtraction		_____ Divide/Division
_____ Absolute Value		_____ Negative Values
_____ Positive Values		_____ Equals
_____ Exponent		_____ Add/Addition

Your Turn
Explain what you are going to learn. Use the sentence starter for support.

I will learn about …

Vocabulary in Context **Picture It!**

Operation A math process
+ Addition
− Subtraction
× Multiplication
÷ Division

Add, Addition, Plus

$$47 + 90 = 137$$

Equals

Subtract, Subtraction, Minus

$$125 - 50 = 75$$

Multiply, Multiplication, Times

$$10 \times 2.5 = 25$$

Divide, Division, Divided By

$$20 \div 4 = 5$$

+, −, ×, and ÷ are all **symbols.**

| Negative values | Positive values |

$$\begin{array}{ccccccccc} -3 & -2 & -1 & 0 & 1 & 2 & 3 & 4 \end{array}$$

Parentheses Tells which operation in an expression to do first

( ) ⟵ **Parentheses**

Absolute Value A number's distance from zero

$|y|$ ⟵ **Absolute Value** of y

Exponent, Power Tells how many times a number is used as a factor

x^2 ⟵ **Exponent**

Scientific Notation A system of writing a number as the product of a power of 10 and a number between 1 and 10

$$2 \times 10^3$$

Talk About It

Talk with a partner to complete these statements about mathematical symbols.

1. I use the symbol + when I want to …

2. I use the ÷ when I want to …

3. I use the symbol − when I want to …

Your Turn

Work in small groups. Discuss the meaning of each of the following symbols: =, $|x|$, x^2, ( ).

Draw a line from each vocabulary term to its symbol.

1. Absolute value
2. Add
3. Divide
4. Equals
5. Exponent
6. Multiply
7. Negative Value
8. Parentheses
9. Positive Value
10. Scientific Notation
11. Subtract

a. $=$
b. $-$
c. x^2
d. -3
e. $\div$
f. $+$
g. $(\ )$
h. 2×10^2
i. $\times$
j. $+5$
k. $|x|$

Talk About It

1. The little 2 in 6^2 is called an …

2. If I want to say *negative 5*, I would use the symbol …

Your Turn
Talk to your partner about ways that might help you remember the meaning of each vocabulary term. Discuss how to use each term in a sentence.

Your Turn

Work with a partner. Write the symbol for addition on an index card. Do the same for subtraction, multiplication, and division. Then listen to your teacher.

Talk and Write About It

Look back at the rating chart on page 5. For each item you ranked as a 2 or 3, make an index card using pictures, numbers, and words. Make a card for any other vocabulary term you need help remembering.

Scientific Notation

A system of writing a number as the product of a power of 10 and a number between 1 and 10

Example: 3×10^4

Absolute Value

A number's distance from zero

Examples: $|6| = 6$
$|-3| = 3$

Produce Language

Write using as many of the vocabulary terms as possible. You may write a separate sentence for each term or combine terms into one question, sentence, or story problem.

Inverse Operations

Essential Question How do you use English to understand and explain inverse operations?

You Will
- Use inverse operations to solve addition and subtraction problems.
- Use inverse operations to solve multiplication and division problems.
- Correctly use vocabulary relating to inverse operations.

Talk About It

Copy each term from Vocabulary in Context on a card. As your teacher reads each term, create three piles of cards.

Step 1 Place terms that you know in **Pile 1.**

Step 2 Place terms you have heard but are not sure what they mean in **Pile 2.**

Step 3 Place terms you do not know in **Pile 3.**

What do you know about each term? Explain, using the sentence frames for support.

Pile 1 I know … means …
Pile 2 I think … means …
Pile 3 I do not know what … means.

addition

operation

divide

Your Turn
Describe what you think you are going to learn. Use the sentence starter for support.

I am going to learn about …

Operation A math process
+ Addition
− Subtraction
× Multiplication
÷ Division

Add, Addition, Plus

$$47 + 90 = 137$$

Equals

Subtract, Subtraction, Minus

$$125 - 50 = 75$$

Multiply, Multiplication, Times

$$10 \times 2.5 = 25$$

Divide, Division, Divided by

$$20 \div 4 = 5$$

Inverse operations Two operations that reverse the effect of each other

Input, Output

Rule: + 3	
Input	*Output*
2	5
3	6
4	7

Talk About It

Talk with a partner to complete these statements.

1 Multiplication is the inverse operation for …

2 Addition is the … for subtraction.

3 If the input is 2 and the rule is × 5, the output is …

Your Turn

Describe how inverse operations work. Share them with your partner.

In math, inverse operations are two operations that undo each other.

Complete the second table.

Rule: × 2	
Input	Output
1	2
2	4
3	6
10	20

Rule: ÷ 2	
Input	Output
2	1
4	___
___	___
___	___

Since dividing by 2 reverses the effect of multiplying by 2,

division and multiplication are _____.

Talk About It
Work with a partner to answer each question.

1 The inverse operation of multiplying by 4 is …

2 The inverse operation of adding 6 is …

3 Maria says that subtraction and division are inverse operations of each other. Is she correct? Why or why not.

Your Turn
Think of a few sentences that describe how an inverse operation reverses the effect on another operation and how you could use these operations in math. Share your ideas with a partner.

Think, Talk, and Write

Your Turn

Complete the rules and tables.

1

Rule: + 5	
Input	Output
1	6
2	7
3	8
4	9

Rule: ____	
Input	Output
6	1
7	2
8	3
9	4

2

Rule: ____	
Input	Output
1	10
2	20
3	30
4	40

Rule: ____	
Input	Output
10	____
20	____
30	____
40	____

Talk and Write About It

Use the vocabulary terms to complete each sentence about inverse operations.

1 Exercise 1 above shows that

Subtracting 5 reverses the effect of

_____ , so they are

_____ operations.

2 Exercise 2 above shows that

_____ reverses the effect of

_____ , so they are

_____ operations.

Produce Language

Use the vocabulary terms on your index cards to write about what you know about inverse operations. If there are things you do not understand, write your questions at the end.

Equivalent Fractions

Essential Question What vocabulary terms do you need to use and understand to talk about simplifying fractions and equivalent fractions?

You Will
- Identify equivalent fractions.
- Find equivalent fractions.
- Simplify fractions.
- Learn vocabulary about equivalent fractions and simplifying fractions.

Talk About It

Rate the following mathematical terms according to the following scale:

1. I have never heard this term before.

2. I have heard this term before, but I don't know how to use it in mathematics.

3. I understand the meaning of this term and know how to use it in mathematics.

_____ Fraction	_____ Whole
_____ Fractional part of	_____ Simplify
_____ Part	_____ Improper Fraction
_____ Equivalent	_____ Numerator
_____ Fraction of the total number of	_____ Denominator
_____ Equivalent Fractions	

Your Turn

Work in pairs or small groups. For each term you labeled 3, compare what you know to be sure you agree on what the term means and how it is used. For each term labeled 2, talk about what you do know or think about that term.

Vocabulary in Context **Picture It!**

Fraction A number that names part of a set or part of a whole

$$\frac{1}{3} \quad \frac{2}{5} \quad \frac{7}{10}$$

 $\frac{2}{3}$

$\frac{2}{3}$ ← Numerator
Denominator

Fractional part of a whole

whole

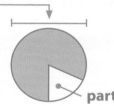

part

Improper fraction A fraction greater than or equal to 1. The numerator is greater than or equal to the denominator.

$$\frac{4}{3} \quad \frac{6}{6}$$

Equivalent Numbers that name the same amount

equivalent fractions:

$$\frac{1}{4} = \frac{2}{8} = \frac{3}{12} = \frac{4}{16}$$

Simplify (a fraction) The process done to get a fraction in its simplest form.

$$\frac{4}{16} = \frac{1}{4}$$

Multiple Product of a given number and a whole number. 3, 6, and 9 are multiples of 3.

Talk About It

Talk with a partner to complete these statements.

1. In the fraction $\frac{5}{8}$, 5 is the …

2. In the fraction $\frac{1}{6}$, 6 is the …

3. $\frac{9}{4}$ is an …

4. 5, 10, 15, and 20 are … of 5.

Your Turn

Work in small groups. Share what you know about each vocabulary term or phrase. Use an index card to make a vocabulary card for each term that you have difficulty with.

Look at each picture below. Think about how it shows the fraction.
Color the last picture to show the fraction labeled.

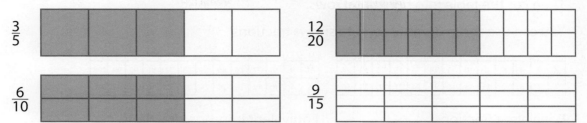

$\frac{3}{5}$

$\frac{12}{20}$

$\frac{6}{10}$

$\frac{9}{15}$

Talk About It

What do you know about fractions? Work with a partner. Use the sentence starters and vocabulary terms to answer each question.

1. In each picture above, the large rectangle is 1 whole.
   Then each small rectangle is a …

2. Each picture shows the same fraction of the whole colored,
   so $\frac{3}{5}$, $\frac{6}{10}$, $\frac{9}{15}$, and $\frac{12}{20}$ are …

3. The fraction that shows how many blocks are circled below is …

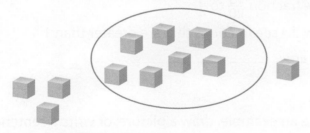

4. This fraction in simplest form is …

Your Turn

Work with a partner. Use the rectangle. Color a fraction of the rectangle.
Name the fraction that you colored. Label the numerator and denominator.

Your Turn

Carefully cut out the Equivalent Fraction Strips on page 97.
Then cut the table into horizontal rows.

You can use these number rows to shows fractions.

2	2	4	6	8	10	12	14	16	18	20	22	24
3	3	6	9	12	15	18	21	24	27	30	33	36

9	9	18	27	36	45	54	63	72	81	90	99	108
4	4	8	12	16	20	24	28	32	36	40	44	48

Equivalent fractions:

$$\frac{2}{3}, \frac{4}{6}, \frac{6}{9}, \frac{8}{12}, \frac{10}{15}$$

Equivalent improper fractions:

$$\frac{9}{4}, \frac{18}{8}, \frac{27}{12}, \frac{36}{16}$$

Talk and Write About It

Use your number rows, the class discussion, your math vocabulary, and the examples above to help you finish each sentence.

1. Place row 3 above row 4. With these rows lined up,

   I see fractions $\frac{3}{4}$, _____ , and _____ .

   These are _____ fractions.

2. I can _____ the fraction $\frac{15}{20}$ to $\frac{3}{4}$.

3. If I put row 4 above row 3, I see fractions that are greater than 1,

   such as $\frac{4}{3}$ and $\frac{8}{6}$. These are _____ .

Produce Language

Work in small groups. Write an example, draw a picture, or write a sentence that will help you understand and use the terms on your vocabulary cards. Then, create your own equivalent fractions and discuss them with a partner.

Fractions, Decimals, and Percents

Essential Question What vocabulary do you need to understand to work with fractions, decimals, and percents?

You Will
- Recognize numbers, including fractions, mixed numbers, decimals, and percents.
- Convert whole numbers, fractions, decimals, and percents.
- Use math vocabulary when discussing and using fractions, mixed numbers, decimals, and percents.

Talk About It

Look at the list of terms below. Place terms you **know, want** to know more about, and those you have **learned** in class into the chart.

decimal	decimal point	mixed number
fraction	equivalent	tenths
numerator	denominator	hundredths
percent	improper fraction	

Know	Want	Learned

Your Turn

Work in pairs or small groups. Discuss what the objectives mean to you.

I know that … means …

Vocabulary in Context **Picture It!**

Fraction A number that names part of a group or part of a whole

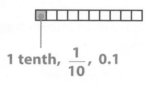

$\dfrac{2}{3}$ ← numerator
denominator

improper fractions   **mixed numbers**

$\dfrac{8}{5}$ $\dfrac{6}{6}$ $3\dfrac{1}{2}$ $1\dfrac{4}{5}$

Decimal A number containing a decimal point

2.42

decimal point

tenths

1 tenth, $\dfrac{1}{10}$, 0.1

hundredth

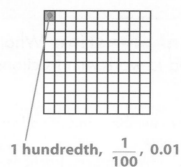

1 hundredth, $\dfrac{1}{100}$, 0.01

Percent Part per 100

3%   65%   100%

Equivalent The same as or is equal to

Talk About It

Talk with a partner to complete these statements.

1. $3\dfrac{7}{10}$ is a …

2. If something is divided into 10 equal parts, each part is called a …

3. 16% means 16 parts per …

Your Turn

Talk about places where you see decimals.

A — One whole unit

B — One whole unit separated into tenths

C — One whole unit separated into hundredths

Use your pencil. Shade one whole unit of square A. Shade one tenth of square B. Shade one hundredth of square C. In square C, shade what you think one thousandth looks like.

Complete the table below to show the amount of each square you shaded. Remember, a percent is a part per 100, so 1% is one hundredth.

Amount Shaded	Written as a Fraction	Written as a Decimal	Written as a Percent
one whole unit	$\frac{1}{1}$	1.0	100%
one tenth	$\frac{1}{10}$		10%
one hundredth			1%
one thousandth			

Talk About It 💬
Use what you have learned to discuss each question.

1. Numbers like $\frac{2}{2}$, $\frac{3}{3}$, and $\frac{12}{12}$ are _____, and each is equivalent to the whole number _____.

2. Numbers like 1.0, 1.00, and 1.000 are _____, and each is equivalent to the whole number _____.

3. Numbers like 10%, 50%, and 100% are _____, and 100% is equivalent to the whole number _____.

Your Turn
One thousand is the whole number 1,000. One thousandth is the decimal 0.001. Talk about how the meaning of the word *ten* changes when you add "th" to the end of the word. Think of other examples where the same thing happens.

You Turn

Use index cards to make vocabulary cards for as many vocabulary terms as you can. Start by writing the term or phrase on the card as shown. Then draw lines to make 4 sections on the card. Label each section.

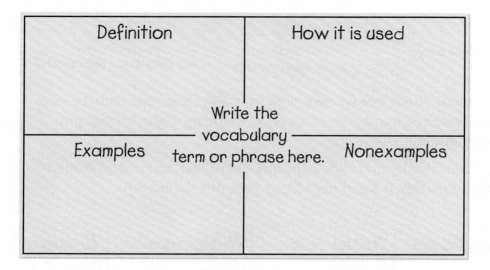

Talk and Write About It

Work in small groups. Compare vocabulary cards. Help each other correct and complete a card for each vocabulary term or phrase listed on the first page of this lesson.

Produce Language

Write about what you have learned about fractions, decimals, and percents. Use as many vocabulary terms and examples as you can.

Ratios and Proportions

You Will
- Identify ratios and proportions.
- Use ratios and proportions to solve problems.
- Use vocabulary terms to talk about ratios and proportions.

Talk About It

Copy each term from Vocabulary in Context on a card.
As your teacher reads each term, create three piles of cards.

Step 1 Place terms that you know in **Pile 1.**

Step 2 Place terms you have heard but are not sure what they mean in **Pile 2.**

Step 3 Place terms you do not know in **Pile 3.**

What do you know about each term? Explain, using the sentence frames for support.

Pile 1 I know … means …
Pile 2 I think … means …
Pile 3 I do not know what … means.

square

ratio

scale

Your Turn

Work in small groups. Discuss each term, sharing what you know with others in your group. Then put each pile in a separate envelope labeled with the number of the pile.

Vocabulary in Context **Picture It!**

Ratio A comparison of two numbers

$$3 \text{ to } 5, \ 3{:}5, \ \frac{3}{5}$$

Proportion An equation that shows that two ratios are equal

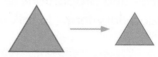

Scale The ratio of the size in a drawing or model to the actual size of the object it represents

Enlarge To make an image larger using a proportion

Reduce To make an image smaller using a proportion

Equilateral triangle A triangle with 3 equal sides

Square A shape with 4 equal sides and 4 right angles

Talk About It

Talk with a partner to complete these statements.

1. Jason wants to change the size of a small picture so it fits in a picture frame that is twice the size of the picture. Jason needs to … the picture.

2. 6:8, $\frac{6}{8}$, and 6 to 8 are all ways to write a ….

3. Two ratios that are equal form a …

Your Turn

Play "What am I?" with a partner. Ask each other questions like these.

- I am made up of two equal ratios. What am I?

- I have four sides of the same length, four right angles, and am a polygon. What am I?

Ratios and proportions are useful when reading a floor plan.

The side of each square represents an actual length of 3 feet.

Room A is 4 squares long. Use a proportion to find the actual length.

$$\frac{1 \text{ square}}{3 \text{ feet}} = \frac{4 \text{ squares}}{? \text{ feet}}$$

Think about the relationship between the ratios.

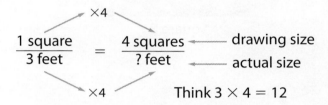

$\times 4$

$$\frac{1 \text{ square}}{3 \text{ feet}} = \frac{4 \text{ squares}}{? \text{ feet}}$$ ⟵ drawing size ⟵ actual size

$\times 4$

Think $3 \times 4 = 12$

The actual length of room A is 12 feet.

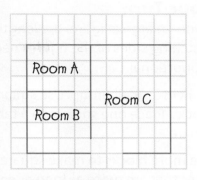

Scale 1 square: 3 feet

Talk About It
Complete each sentence.

1 When you look at a floor plan, the … shows the … of the length on the drawing to the actual length.

2 To find the actual length represented on a floor plan, set up a …

3 The length and width of room B are the same, so room B is in the shape of a …

Your Turn
Work in a small group. Look at the map at the right. Talk about how a map is like the floor plan. Discuss how you can use the scale to find actual distances.

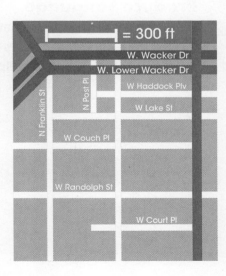

= 300 ft

W. Wacker Dr
W. Lower Wacker Dr
W Haddock Plv
W Lake St
W Couch Pl
W Randolph St
W Court Pl

N Franklin St
N Post Pl

Ratios and Proportions

Your Turn

If you enlarge a figure, the lengths of the matching sides of the figures need to be proportional.

Work in a small group. Use square pattern blocks. Place one square on a table. This is square A.

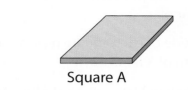

Square A

Use more blocks to make square B so it has sides that are twice as long as square A.

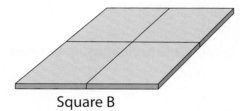

Square B

$$\frac{\text{bottom side of square A}}{\text{bottom side of square B}} \longrightarrow \frac{1}{2}$$

$$\frac{\text{left side of square A}}{\text{left side of square B}} \longrightarrow \frac{1}{2}$$

Talk and Write About It

Use your squares or the drawings above to complete each sentence starter.

1. In squares A and B, the _____ of the lengths of the bottom sides is $\frac{1}{2}$. This can also be written as _____ or _____ .

2. In squares A and B, the _____ of the lengths of the left sides is $\frac{1}{2}$. This can also be written as _____ or _____ .

3. If you write $\frac{1}{2} = \frac{1}{2}$, you have written a _____ .

4. Because the ratios of the matching sides make a proportion, you have _____ square A to form square B.

Produce Language

Work in a small group. Use pattern blocks to enlarge an equilateral triangle. Write about the two triangles you formed. Use the sentence starters in Talk and Write About It to help you.

Unit Rates

Essential Question How do you use pictures, numbers, and terms to talk about unit rates?

You Will
- Use ratios and proportions to find unit rates.
- Use ratios and proportions to find unit prices and the better buy.
- Use proper vocabulary when talking about ratios, proportions, and unit rates.

Talk About It

Rate the following mathematical terms according to the following scale:

1. I have never heard this term before.

2. I have heard this term before, but I don't know how to use it in mathematics.

3. I understand the meaning of this term and know how to use it in mathematics.

   _____ Table

   _____ Ounce (oz)

   _____ Inch (in.)

   _____ Minute (min)

   _____ Average rate of (speed)

   _____ Proportion

   _____ Second (sec)

   _____ Rate of change

   _____ Unit rate

Your Turn
Explain what you are going to learn. Use the sentence starter for support.

I will learn about …

Vocabulary in Context Picture It!

Table

Distance (ft)	10	20	30	40
Time (min)	2	4	6	8

Ratio A comparison of two numbers   3 to 5, 3:5, $\frac{3}{5}$

Proportion Two equal ratios
$$\frac{3}{5} = \frac{6}{10}$$

Rate A ratio that involves different types of units

Unit rate A rate in which the second term is 1 unit of measure, such as 40 miles per gallon.

Unit price A unit rate that gives the cost per unit of measurement $3 per square foot

Speed Unit rate that gives the distance per unit of time
    45 miles per hour

Rate of change A rate that shows how one number changes in relation to another number

Inch (in.) Unit of length;
    12 inches = 1 foot

Second (sec) Unit of time;
    60 seconds = 1 minute

Minute (min) Unit of time;
    60 minutes = 1 hour

Ounce (oz) Unit of weight;
    16 ounces = 1 pound

Talk About It

Work in pairs or small groups. Use the sentence starters to talk about the vocabulary terms.

1. The ratio "2 ft per minute" can be written as $\frac{2\,ft}{1\,min}$ or $\frac{2\,ft}{min}$ and is called a …

2. Rates sometimes involve units of time. Some units of time are …

3. Rates sometimes involve units of length. Some units of length are …

Your Turn

Work in a small group. Which of these ratios is a rate? Give reasons for your answers.

a. $\frac{6\,in.}{10\,in.}$ b. 6 in. : 2 min   c. 5 miles per hour

1,350 miles in 3 hours

$$\frac{1{,}350 \text{ miles}}{3 \text{ hours}}$$

80 miles in 2 hours

$$\frac{80 \text{ miles}}{2 \text{ hours}}$$

280 miles in 4 hours

$$\frac{280 \text{ miles}}{4 \text{ hours}}$$

Question: How fast does each travel in miles per hour?

$$\frac{1{,}350}{3} = \frac{?}{1}$$

$$\frac{80}{2} = \frac{?}{1}$$

$$\frac{280}{4} = \frac{?}{1}$$

$$\frac{1{,}350 \div 3}{3 \div 3} = \frac{450}{1}$$

$$\frac{80 \div 2}{2 \div 2} = \frac{40}{1}$$

$$\frac{280 \div 4}{4 \div 4} = \frac{70}{1}$$

450 miles per hour

40 miles per hour

70 miles per hour

Talk About It

Work in pairs or small groups. Use the vocabulary terms to complete each sentence starter.

1. The plane travels 1,350 miles in 3 hours. 1,350 miles to 3 hours is a … and also a …

2. The car travels at 40 miles per hour. 40 miles per hour is a … rate and also the …

3. The speed of the train is …

Your Turn

The table shows how many feet of rope a machine can make in different amounts of time.

Rope Production

Minutes	5	10	15	20
Feet	200	400	600	800

The table shows a … of 200 feet every 5 minutes

The … for this machine is 40 feet per minute.

Your Turn

Look at the advertisement at the right. Do you really save 20¢?

Yes, you spend 20¢ less, but you get fewer blueberries.

To compare these prices, you need to find each unit price, or price per ounce.

Frozen Blueberries
Store Brand $2.40   16 oz
National Brand $2.60   20 oz

Save 20¢

Store Brand Unit Price

$$\frac{\$2.40}{16\ oz} = \frac{?}{1\ oz}$$

Unit price = 15¢ per ounce

National Brand Unit Price

$$\frac{\$2.60}{20\ oz} = \frac{?}{1\ oz}$$

Unit price = 13¢ per ounce

If you bought 20 ounces of each, the store brand would cost $3.00, and the national brand would cost $2.60. The national brand is a better buy.

Talk and Write About It

Work in pairs to complete each sentence starter.

Canned Corn   **Save 60¢**

Store Brand 15 oz $0.60
      Unit price 4¢ per oz

National Brand 30 oz $1.20
      Unit price 4¢ per oz

1. If you only look at the prices in the ad, does it seem like you are saving

   money? _____

2. What is the difference between the store brand and the national brand?

   _____

3. Each product has a _____ of 4¢ per ounce.

4. How would you decide which brand to buy?

   _____

Produce Language

Work in small groups. Write about what you learned. Use the sentence starters throughout the lesson for support.

Patterns

Essential Question What vocabulary terms do you need to know and use to learn about patterns in mathematics?

You Will
- Analyze patterns.
- Recognize the rule for extending a pattern and extend that pattern.
- Recognize linear relationships.
- Use vocabulary terms to talk about patterns and relationships.

Talk About It

Copy each term from Vocabulary in Context on a card. As your teacher reads each term, create three piles of cards.

Step 1 Place terms that you know in **Pile 1.**

Step 2 Place terms that you have heard but are not sure what they mean in **Pile 2.**

Step 3 Place terms you do not know in **Pile 3.**

What do you know about each term? Explain, using the sentence frames for support.

Pile 1 I know … means …
Pile 2 I think … means …
Pile 3 I do not know what … means.

table

graph

pattern

Your Turn
Work in pairs. Use the sentence starters in your discussions.

I want to learn more about …

I think it means …

Vocabulary in Context Picture It!

Pattern

Number pattern

2, 4, 6, 8, 10, 12, …

1, 2, 3, 1, 2, 3, 1, 2, 3, …

Rule A set of directions

Table

Distance (mi)	100	200	300	400
Time (hours)	2	4	6	8

Graph

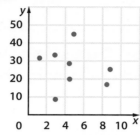

Value The number associated with something

Represents Stands for

Linear relationship A relationship whose graph is a set of points that lie on a line

Talk About It

Work in small groups. Share information about your terms in pile 3. Listen carefully to what others say about the terms you have in piles 1 and 2. Use the sentence starters.

1. "Multiply by 4" is a …

2. Numbers arranged by following a rule form a … and an example is …

3. One way to display information is in a … and an example is …

Your Turn

Think about what you know and what you have heard about the vocabulary terms. Write or draw pictures on your index cards to help you remember what the terms mean.

Find a rule for each pattern below. Then extend the pattern.

Pattern 1: 2, 5, 8, 11, 14, …

Think: How do the numbers change?

$$2, \quad 5, \quad 8, \quad 11, \quad 14, \dots$$
$$+3 \quad +3 \quad +3 \quad +3$$

Rule: To get to the next number, add 3.

Extend the pattern: The next number is 14 + 3, or 17. Then 17 + 3, or 20, and so on.

Pattern 2: 1, 6, 11, 1, 6, 11, 1, 6, 11, 1, …

Look at the pattern. If you see the same group of numbers over and over, the pattern repeats.

$$1, 6, 11, 1, 6, 11, 1, 6, 11, 1, \dots$$

Rule: Repeat 1, 6, 11.

Extend the pattern: 6, 11, 1, …

Talk About It

Matt wrote this on the board: 5, 9, 13, 17, 21, 25, …

Sylvia wrote this on the board: 3, 6, 9, 3, 6, 9, 3, 6, 9, 3, 6, …

Work in pairs. Use the vocabulary terms to complete each sentence starter.

1 On the board, Matt wrote a …

2 Matt said he added 4 to get to the next number. "Add 4" is …

3 The next number in Matt's pattern would be …

4 Sylvia's … repeats.

5 The part of Sylvia's … that repeats is …

6 The next three numbers in Sylvia's pattern would be …

Your Turn

Work in pairs. One student makes up a number pattern by adding the same amount each time. The other student tries to guess the rule and tell what number comes next in the pattern. Then switch roles.

Repeat the activity, but make up a number pattern that repeats.

Your Turn

The pairs of numbers in this table have a pattern.

Rule: Add 2 to *x* to get *y*.

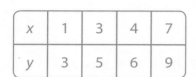

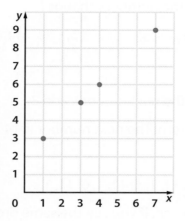

There is also a pattern in the graph of the pairs of numbers.

All of the points lie on a line. This means that the values in the table represent a linear relationship.

Talk and Write About It

Complete each sentence about the pattern shown in the table.

1. The _____ for the pattern is to add 2 to the value of *x* to find

    the _____ of *y*.

2. Look at the points on the graph. If these points were connected,

    you would get a _____.

3. In the graph of a linear relationship, the points lie on a _____.

Produce Language

Work in pairs or small groups. Use the table and the graph to talk and write about what you have learned using lesson vocabulary.

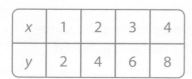

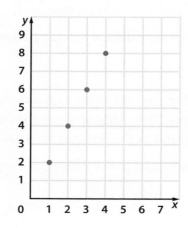

Expressions

Essential Question What vocabulary terms do you need to learn about expressions with variables?

You Will
- Read linear expressions.
- Write linear expressions.
- Use correct terms when reading and talking about expressions.

Talk About It

Rate the mathematical terms according to the following scale:

1. I have never heard of this term before.

2. I have heard this term before, but I don't know how to use it in mathematics.

3. I understand the meaning of this term and know how to use it in mathematics.

_____ Expression   _____ Table

_____ Estimate   _____ Variable

_____ Symbol

Your Turn

Explain what you are going to learn. Use the sentence starter for support.

I will learn about …

Vocabulary in Context Picture It!

Expression

2 + 4 $n + 523$

Estimate A good guess or approximate value rather than an exact number

Symbol

n $\angle$ $+$

Variable A symbol that represents a number

$5n$ ◄——— variable

Table

Distance (miles)	100	200	300	400
Time (hours)	2	4	6	8

Talk About It

Work with a partner to complete the sentences below.

1. $m + 5$
   The '+' is a ... in the expression.

2. A ... is used to organize data or information.

3. A variable is used to ... a number in an expression.

Your Turn

Work in small groups. Talk about how these terms are related.

Do You Understand?

An expression often includes an operation symbol. There are different ways to show an operation.

Add 3 and *n*: $3 + n$ $n + 3$

Subtract 3 from *n*: $n - 3$

Subtract *n* from 3: $3 - n$

Multiply 3 and *n*: $3 \times n$ $3n$ $3(n)$ $3 \cdot n$ $3 * n$

Divide *n* by 4: $n \div 4$ $\dfrac{n}{4}$ n/4

Divide 4 by *n*: $4 \div n$ $\dfrac{4}{n}$ 4/n

Talk About It

Match each sentence with the correct expression. Not all of the expressions will be used.

1 Add *n* and 6. _____

2 Multiply 6 and *n*. _____

3 Divide *n* by 6. _____

4 Subtract *n* from 6. _____

5 Find the sum of *p* and 5. _____

6 Find the product of 5 and *p*. _____

7 Find the value of 5 divided by *p*. _____

8 Find the number 5 less than *p*. _____

a. $n \div 6$

b. $n - 6$

c. $n + 6$

d. $6n$

e. $6 - n$

f. 6/n

g. $p - 5$

h. $p + 5$

i. $5p$

j. $\dfrac{p}{5}$

k. $5 - p$

l. $5 \div p$

Your Turn

Work in small groups. Compare your answers using as many vocabulary terms as you can to talk about expressions.

Think, Talk, and Write

Your Turn

Parentheses are used when a negative number is part of an expression.

Expression in Words	Math Expression
-3 more than b	$b + (-3)$ or $-3 + b$
-4 less than n	$n - (-4)$
m divided by -2	$m \div (-2)$ or $m/(-2)$
6 times $-e$	$6(-e)$ or $6 \times (-e)$

Complete the table below.

Expression in Words	Math Expression
v plus -9	
	$3(-a)$
p divided by -2	
	$a - (-1)$

Talk and Write About It

Complete each sentence.

1. _____ are made up of numbers, variables, and symbols.

2. n is a _____ and it represents a _____ .

3. $(-8)n$ means _____ .

4. The expression that means subtract -8 from c is _____ .

5. To find the quotient in an expression, the symbol I will use is _____ .

6. The order in which I _____ two numbers or _____ two numbers does not change the answer.

Produce Language

Use index cards to make Expression Cards, and list as many examples as possible.

Evaluating Expressions

Essential Question What vocabulary terms do you need to know in order to learn about evaluating expressions?

You Will

- Read and understand algebraic expressions.
- Evaluate expressions using substitution.
- Use correct terms when discussing how to evaluate expressions.

Talk About It

Look at the list of terms below. Place terms you **know, want** to know more about, and those you have **learned** into the chart.

evaluate	variable	multiply/multiplication
expression	exponent	add/addition
symbol	key	subtract/subtraction

Know	Want	Learned

Your Turn

Work in a small group and compare your charts. Talk about the terms you wrote in the Know column. You may want to make notes about questions to ask during class discussion.

Vocabulary in Context Picture It!

Expression

$$4 \times 7 \qquad \frac{25}{n}$$

Variable A symbol that represents a number

$$b \quad x \quad n$$

Evaluate To find the value of

base

$$9^3 = 9 \times 9 \times 9$$

exponent   **factor**

Substitute To put something in place of another thing

$$n + 1$$

Substitute 4 for n.

$$4 + 1$$

Least to greatest

$$0.1, \frac{1}{2}, 1, 1\frac{1}{2}, 2.9$$

Greatest to least

$$2.9, 1\frac{1}{2}, 1, \frac{1}{2}, 0.1$$

Talk About It

Work in pairs. Use the vocabulary terms to complete each sentence starter.

1. When I … the expression $3 + 8$, I find the value of $3 + 8$.

2. The numbers 0.02, 0.2, 2.0, and 2.2 are ordered from …

3. In the expression 2^4, the … is 4. The 4 tells you to use 2 as a … four times.

4. The symbol • in the expression $3 \cdot 6$ means to …

5. In the … $x + 5$, the letter x is a …

Your Turn

Work in small groups. Talk about ways that can help you remember the meaning of each vocabulary term.

To evaluate an expression, substitute a number for the variable and find the value of the expression.

Evaluate		Substitute		Find the value
$9n$ for $n = 5$	→	9×5	→	45
$1.25 + p$ for $p = 0.25$	→	$1.25 + 0.25$	→	_____
$\dfrac{x}{2}$ for $x = -14$	→	$\dfrac{-14}{2}$	→	_____
$10 - y$ for $y = 24$	→	$10 - 24$	→	_____

Talk About It

Work in pairs to complete each exercise or sentence.

1. When you … an expression, you find the value of the expression.

2. Substitute a number for a … to evaluate an expression.

3. The value of $b - 9$ when $b = 23$ is …

4. The value of $8x$ when $x = 4$ is …

5. The value of $\dfrac{m}{3}$ when $m = 24$ is …

6. The value of $\dfrac{m}{3}$ when $m = 21$ is …

7. Look at Exercises 5 and 6. What happens to the value of the expression when you change the value of the variable?

Your Turn

Work with a partner. One partner writes an expression, and the other partner names a value for the variable and evaluates the expression. The first partner checks that the evaluation is correct.

Your Turn

Evaluate each expression. Write the value.

Evaluate	$l \div 2$ for $l = 8$	$3a$ for $a = -4$	$\frac{r}{5}$ for $r = 1.25$	$b \bullet 2$ for $b = 1$
Value	4			
Variable	l	a	r	b

Evaluate	$-9 + v$ for $v = -7$	$1 - a$ for $a = 0.2$	$4e$ for $e = 2$	$\frac{1}{i}$ for $i = 2$
Value				
Variable	v	a	e	i

Talk and Write About It

Work in pairs to complete each exercise.

1 Order the values you found in the tables above from least to greatest.

_____

2 Fill in the table below by ordering the values you found from least to greatest. Below each value, write the variable that was used in the expression.

Value	-16						4	
Variable	v						l	

3 What word is spelled out in the second row of the table above? _____

Some expressions have more than one variable. Evaluate each expression for $n = 4$ and $p = 8$.

4 $n + p$ _____

5 $p \div n$ _____

6 $n \bullet p$ _____

Produce Language

Pretend you are teaching someone how to evaluate expressions. Write about what you would show and tell them.

Linear Equations

Essential Question How do you discuss solving linear equations using words, symbols, tables, and graphs?

You Will
- Represent linear equations using words, symbols, tables, and graphs.
- Use rules to write and solve linear equations.
- Understand and use key terms related to linear equations.

Talk About It

As your teacher reads each mathematical term, rate the term according to the following scale:

1. I have never heard of this term before.

2. I have heard this term before, but I don't know how to use it in mathematics.

3. I understand the meaning of this term and know how to use it in mathematics.

_____ Table	_____ Equation
_____ Pattern	_____ Rule
_____ Number Pattern	_____ Linear Equation
_____ Graph	

Your Turn

Describe what you think you are going to learn. Use the sentence starter for support.

I will learn about …

Vocabulary in Context Picture It!

Table A chart with columns and rows that display information

x	y
0	0
2	4
4	8

Pattern A set of numbers, shapes, or objects arranged according to a rule

2, 5, 8, 11, 14, 17, 20

Number pattern

2, 4, 8, 16, 32

Rule: Multiply by 2.
Equation: $y = 2x$

Linear equation An equation whose graph is a straight line

$$y = x + 2$$

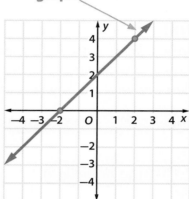

Talk About It

Work with a partner to complete each sentence.

1 A display of information in columns and rows is called a …

2 A sentence that shows that two expressions are equal is called an …

3 A set of shapes or numbers that follow a rule forms a …

4 A written statement that describes a pattern is called a …

Your Turn

Think about how you could describe the terms in this lesson. Share your ideas with a partner.

The information below shows different ways to represent linear equations.

Table	Graph

Table

Fill in the table.

x	y
−3	−2
−1	0
1	2
3	4
5	

Graph

Mark all of the points from the table on the graph.

Rule and Linear Equation	Words

Rule and Linear Equation

Rule: _____

Linear Equation: _____

Words

Circle the vocabulary terms.

The rule is that you add one to a number to find another number.

The graph of this linear equation is a straight line.

Talk About It

Complete the sentences.

1 An equation that describes the graph of a line is called a …

2 A … can be used to predict values in a table.

3 A set of numbers arranged according to a rule is called a …

Your Turn

Write another sentence that belongs in the Words part of the chart above.

Your Turn

Think of a rule that describes a pattern. Fill in the information below to show different ways to represent the pattern as a linear equation.

Table	Graph

x	y

Rule and Linear Equation	Words

Rule: _____

Linear equation: _____

Talk and Write About It

Complete the sentences using vocabulary terms that you have learned about linear equations in this lesson.

1. A line shows the graph of a _____ .

2. You can use a rule to describe a _____ .

3. To form a sentence that states that two expressions have the same value is to write an _____ .

Produce Language

Write about what you learned. Use the information you filled in and the sentence starters throughout this lesson for support.

Slope

Essential Question How do you explain the slope of a line using a picture, numbers, and words?

You Will
- Understand that slope is a measure of a line's steepness and that it shows a constant rate of change.
- Identify the slope of a line and its *y*-intercept from the equation of the line.
- Understand and use new terms related to slope.

Talk About It

Tear out the Slope Four Corner Activity on pages 99–101.

Each corner of the room has a number and an equation that represents the graph of a line.

Step 1 Go to a corner of the room. Find the box that matches the corner number. Write the equation of that corner inside the box.

Step 2 Look at the graphs on page 101. Find the graph that represents the equation. Cut out and glue the graph that you think matches the equation in the box.

Repeat Steps 1 and 2 for each corner of the room.

Your Turn

Talk about what you are going to learn. Use the sentence starter below.

I am going to learn about …

Slope A measure of how steep a line is

Constant rate The rate of change between points on a straight line measured by the slope of the line

y-intercept The value of y where a line crosses the y-axis

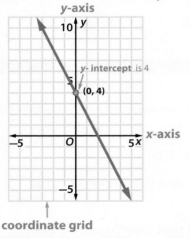

coordinate grid

The line has a **positive slope.** It **increases** from left to right.

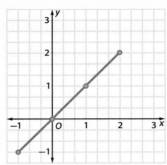

The line has a **negative slope.** It **decreases** from left to right.

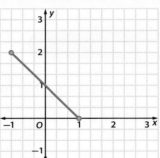

Talk About It

Work with another student to complete the statements.

1. The … is a measure of how steep a line is.

2. If a line goes up from left to right, it …

3. The value of y on the coordinate grid where a line crosses the y-axis is called the …

Your Turn

Think about how you could describe the terms in this lesson. Share your ideas with a partner.

Look at the information in the table and the graph of the line.

Linear Equation	Slope	y-intercept	Coordinates
$y = \frac{1}{2}x + 3$	$\frac{1}{2}$	3	(−2, 2) (0, 3) (2, 4)

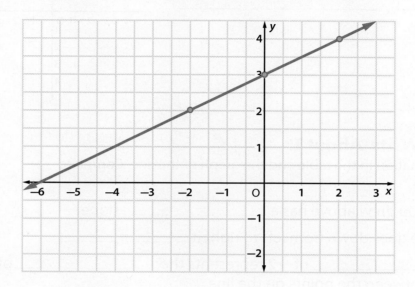

Talk About It

Think about the relationship between the information in the table and the line. Use vocabulary terms to complete the sentence starters.

1. The line shown above has a ... slope.

2. The slope of $\frac{1}{2}$ represents the ... of change between the points on the line.

3. At the point (0, 3) on the graph of the line above, the value of y is 3. This is the ...

4. $y = -4x + 1$

   The ... of this line is −4.

Your Turn

Think about the terms used in this lesson and what they mean. Explain them to a partner.

Your Turn

Complete the information in the table. Then graph the line.

Linear Equation	Slope	y-intercept	Coordinates
$y = -2x + 1$	_____	_____	(−1, 3) (0, 1) (2, −3)

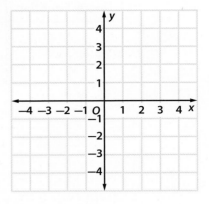

Talk and Write About It

Use the information in the table and the graph of the line. Complete each sentence.

1. The line you drew above has a _____ slope.

2. As the line goes down from left to right it _____.

3. The _____ of −2 represents the _____ of change between the points on the line.

4. The _____ on the graph of the line is 1.

Produce Language

Pretend you are teaching someone how to graph a line and find the slope. Use vocabulary terms to write about what you would show and tell them.

Angles and Lines

Essential Question What terms do you need to know and use in order to understand angles and lines?

You Will
- Identify adjacent angles, complementary angles, and supplementary angles.
- Identify and explain the relationships of angles formed by intersecting lines.
- Identify and explain the relationships of angles formed when parallel lines are cut by a third line.
- Use correct terms when discussing angles and lines.

Talk About It

Write each vocabulary term below on an index card. As your teacher reads each word, create three piles.

degree

Adjacent Angles	Intersecting Lines
Angle	Alternate Exterior Angles
Complementary Angles	Alternate Interior Angles
Congruent Angles	Supplementary Angles
Corresponding Angles	Vertical Angles
parallel lines	vertex
degree	ray

Pile 1: I know what this term means.

Pile 2: I have heard of this term, but I am not sure how it is used in mathematics.

Pile 3: I have not heard of this term.

Your Turn

Talk about what you think you are going to learn. Use the sentence starter for support.

I am going to learn about …

Vocabulary in Context Picture It!

Angle ∠MNP

ray →
vertex →

Adjacent angles

∠ABD and ∠DBC

Degree Unit of measure of angles
Symbol: °

Congruent angles

Complementary angles Two angles whose measures add up to 90°

Supplementary angles Two angles whose measures add up to 180°

Intersecting lines

Parallel lines

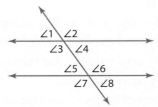

Corresponding angles
∠1 and ∠5   ∠2 and ∠6
∠3 and ∠7   ∠4 and ∠8

Vertical angles
∠1 and ∠4   ∠5 and ∠8
∠2 and ∠3   ∠6 and ∠7

Alternate exterior angles
∠1 and ∠8   ∠2 and ∠7

Alternate interior angles
∠3 and ∠6   ∠4 and ∠5

Talk About It

Talk with a partner. Complete the sentences.

1. The point where two rays meet is called the …

2. An angle is measured in …

3. When a set of parallel lines is cut by a third line, … angles are formed.

Your Turn

Think about the terms you put in Piles 1, 2, and 3. For each index card you made, draw a picture and add a label. Share your cards with your partner.

You can use a ruler to draw parallel lines. You can also use the ruler to draw another line that intersects, or cuts across, the parallel lines.

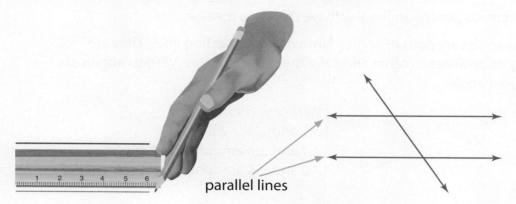

parallel lines

Talk About It

Work in pairs or small groups to discuss angles and lines. Use the sentence starters.

1. If two parallel lines are cut by a third line, then 4 pairs of ... angles are formed.

2. Angles that share a side but do not overlap are ...

3. Two angles whose measures add up to 90° are ... angles.

4. Two lines that have one point in common are ... lines.

5. If two parallel lines are cut by a third line, two pairs of alternate ... angles and two pairs of alternate ... angles are formed.

6. Two angles whose measures add up to 180° are ... angles.

Your Turn

On a separate sheet of paper, use a ruler to draw two parallel lines. Draw a third line that intersects the parallel lines. Number your angles in the same way as the angles are numbered on page 50. Talk about the angles you drew with a partner.

Your Turn

Read about congruent angles and vertical angles below.

Congruent angles are angles that have the same measure.

Vertical angles are pairs of angles formed by intersecting lines. They are directly opposite each other and have the same measure. Vertical angles are congruent angles.

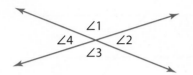

Pairs of vertical angles:
∠1 and ∠3, ∠2 and ∠4
∠1 and ∠3 are congruent angles.
∠2 and ∠4 are congruent angles.

Talk and Write About It

Use vocabulary terms and the parallel lines and angles you drew on page 51 to complete each sentence.

①　A protractor is used to measure angles. Use a protractor to measure the angles you drew. The measures of the angles are:

∠1: _____; ∠2: _____; ∠3: _____; ∠4: _____;
∠5: _____; ∠6: _____; ∠7: _____; ∠8: _____.

②　In my drawing, ∠1 and ∠5 are _____ angles. Are these angles congruent? _____

③　In my drawing, ∠1 and ∠2 are _____ angles. Are these angles congruent? _____

④　In my drawing, ∠1 and ∠8 are _____ angles. Are these angles congruent? _____

⑤　In my drawing, ∠5 and ∠8 are _____ angles. Are these angles congruent? _____

⑥　In my drawing, ∠3 and ∠6 are _____ angles. Are these angles congruent? _____

Produce Language

Place the three piles of index cards on the table. Write one or more sentences to explain what you learned about each vocabulary term. Share your sentences with a partner.

Attributes of Polygons

Essential Question What terms do you need to know and use in order to learn about congruent and similar shapes?

You Will
- Describe polygons by the number of sides and angles.
- Recognize congruent and similar shapes.
- Use and understand terms that describe attributes of polygons.

Talk About It

Copy each term from Vocabulary in Context on a card. Create three piles of cards.

Step 1 Place terms that you know in **Pile 1.**

Step 2 Place terms that you have heard of, but are not sure how they are used in mathematics, in **Pile 2.**

Step 3 Place terms you do not know in **Pile 3.**

Explain what you know about each word, using the sentence frames for support.

Pile 1 I know … means … .

Pile 2 I think … means … .

Pile 3 I do not know what … means.

figure

congruent

right angle

Your Turn
Describe what you think you are going to learn. Use the sentence starter for support.

I am going to learn about …

Vocabulary in Context **Picture It!**

Figure A **shape** or **model**

Angle

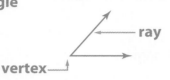

ray

vertex

Polygon A figure with straight sides and angles

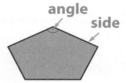

angle

side

A **triangle** has 3 sides.

A **quadrilateral** has 4 sides.

A **pentagon** has 5 sides.

A **hexagon** has 6 sides.

Square   **Rectangle**

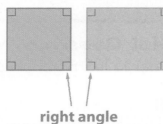

right angle

Trapezoid

Congruent   **Similar**

Talk About It

Talk with a partner. Complete the sentences.

1 A … is a shape or model.

2 Two figures are … when they have the same size and shape.

3 A … is a corner or point where two rays meet.

Your Turn

Think about the vocabulary terms you wrote on the index cards. Write or draw on the back of each card to show what these terms mean.

Match each shape with the correct name.

1.

_____

2.

_____

a. rectangle

b. trapezoid

c. square

d. triangle

e pentagon

f. hexagon

g. quadrilateral

3.

_____

4.

_____

5.

_____

6.

_____

7.

_____

Talk About It

Write the name of the polygon. Then tell how many sides and angles it has. Use the sentence starters for support.

The name of this figure is …

It has … sides and … angles.

Shape	Number of Sides	Number of Angles
_____		
_____		
_____		

Your Turn

Choose a shape. Draw a shape that is similar to the shape you chose. Tell your partner about the shapes. Use vocabulary terms to explain how they are the same and how they are different.

Your Turn

Make shape cards. Draw one shape on a card. Write the name of the shape on the card.

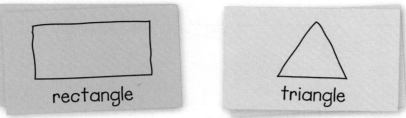

Talk and Write About It 🗨 ✏

Look at the figures on your cards. Complete each sentence.

1. The polygon with 5 sides is called a _____.

2. The polygon with 4 _____ angles and 4 equal sides is called a
   _____.

3. The polygon with 3 sides and 3 angles is called a _____.

4. The polygon with 6 angles is called a _____.

5. A rectangle is like a trapezoid because they each have _____
   sides and _____ angles.

6. A rectangle is different from a trapezoid because a rectangle has four
   _____.

Produce Language

Work with a partner. Look at the cards you created for each shape. Name the shape. Write whether your shape and your partner's shape are congruent or similar.

Coordinate Plane

Essential Question How do you explain and understand *x*- and *y*-coordinates on the coordinate plane?

You Will
- Identify points on a Cartesian coordinate plane.
- Plot points on a Cartesian coordinate plane.
- Use the correct terms when talking about points on a coordinate plane.

Talk About It

Copy each term from Vocabulary in Context on a card. Create three piles of cards.

Step 1 Place terms that you know in **Pile 1.**

Step 2 Place terms that you have heard, but are not sure what they mean, in **Pile 2.**

Step 3 Place terms that you do not know in **Pile 3.**

Explain what you know about each word, using the sentence frames for support.

Pile 1 I know … means …

Pile 2 I think … means …

Pile 3 I do not know what … means.

polygon

origin

vertex

Your Turn
Talk about what you think you are going to learn. Use the sentence starter for support.

I think I am going to learn about …

Vocabulary in Context Picture It!

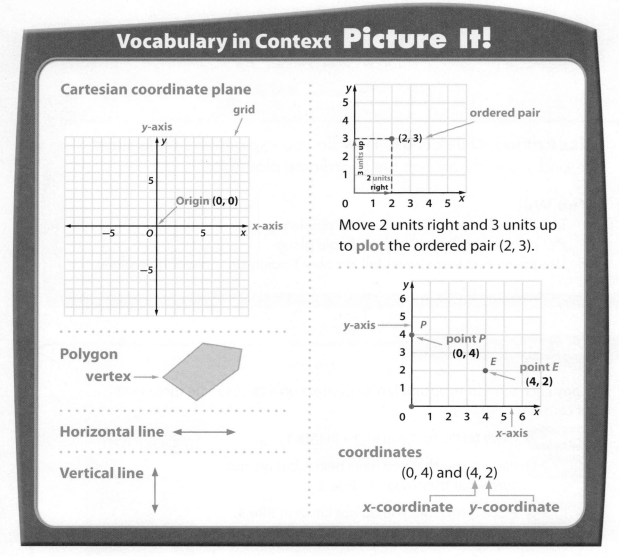

Cartesian coordinate plane

grid
y-axis
Origin (0, 0)
x-axis

Polygon
vertex

Horizontal line

Vertical line

ordered pair
(2, 3)
3 units up
2 units right

Move 2 units right and 3 units up
to **plot** the ordered pair (2, 3).

y-axis
point P
(0, 4)
point E
(4, 2)
x-axis

coordinates
(0, 4) and (4, 2)
x-coordinate   y-coordinate

Talk About It

Use vocabulary terms to complete each sentence.

1 Lines that are drawn up and down are called ... lines.

2 A point where two sides of a polygon meet is called a ...

3 When you locate the place for an ordered pair, you ... that point.

Your Turn

Work in pairs. Talk about the vocabulary terms you put in Pile 2 with your
partner. Use the pictures above to find the meanings of those terms.

Use the grid below to complete the sentences in Talk About It.

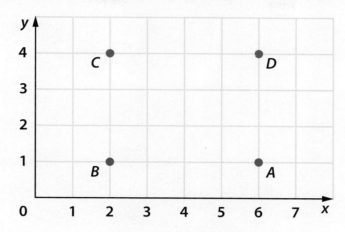

Talk About It

Work in pairs. Use the points on the grid above and the vocabulary terms to complete each sentence.

1. A coordinate … is a grid made of horizontal and … lines.

2. (2, 1) is an … pair.
   In (2, 1), the 2 is the … and 1 is the …

3. The … is located at (0, 0).

4. If you draw lines on the grid to connect A to B, B to C, C to D, and D to A, the figure you have drawn is a …

5. Point A is one … of the figure ABCD.

Your Turn

Work in pairs. Draw figure ABCD on the grid at the top of the page. Write the ordered pair at each vertex. Then use your answers from Talk About It to write labels on the grid.

Your Turn

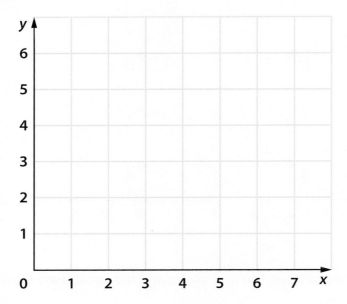

Step 1 Plot each point: (4, 5); (2, 1); (6, 2).

Step 2 Connect the points to make a polygon. What shape did you make?

Talk and Write About It

Discuss each sentence starter with a partner. Then use as many vocabulary terms as possible to complete each sentence.

1. A coordinate plane is a grid that is made up of

_____.

2. To locate a point on a coordinate plane for an ordered pair, start at

_____.

3. To locate a point for the ordered pair (3, 5),

_____.

Produce Language

Look at the cards you put in Piles 2 and 3. Write a sentence to explain what you learned about each vocabulary term.

Transformations

Essential Question How do you use pictures, numbers, and words to talk about transformations?

You Will
- Describe translations, rotations, and reflections on two-dimensional shapes.
- Write new coordinates that show a translation, reflection, and rotation.
- Understand and use key terms related to transformations.

Talk About It

Rate the following mathematical terms according to the following scale:

1. I have never heard of this term before.

2. I have heard this term before, but I don't know how to use it in mathematics.

3. I understand the meaning of this term and know how to use it in mathematics.

_____ Transformation   _____ Coordinate Grid

_____ Translation (slide)   _____ Coordinates

_____ Rotation (turn)   _____ Vertex/Vertices

_____ Reflection (flip)   _____ *x*-axis

_____ Rule   _____ *y*-axis

_____ *x*-coordinate   _____ *y*-coordinate

Your Turn

Describe what you think you will learn in this lesson. Use the sentence starters for support.

I think … means …

An example of a … might be a …

Vocabulary in Context **Picture It!**

Transformation A change to a figure.

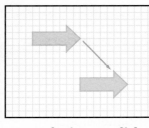

translation or **slide**

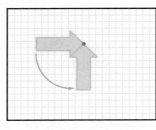

rotation or **turn**

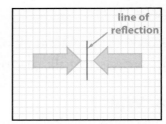

line of reflection

reflection or **flip**

Rule A set of instructions.

Coordinate grid

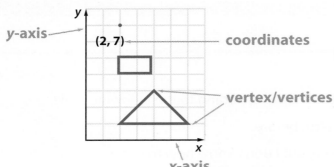

y-axis

(2, 7) — coordinates

vertex/vertices

x-axis

x-coordinate

(2, 7)

y-coordinate

Talk About It

Talk with a partner. Complete the sentences.

1. Another term for a slide is a …

2. The … known as a flip is also called a …

3. Another name for a turn is a …

Your Turn

Tell your partner how a reflection is different from a translation.

You can do transformations on a figure on the coordinate plane by using a rule and the coordinates of the figure.

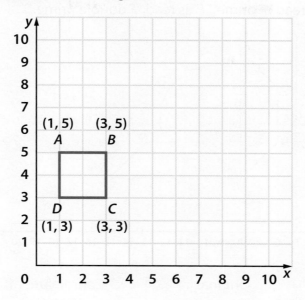

Step 1 Rule: Add 5 to each *x*-coordinate and add 2 to each *y*-coordinate. After the rule is used for point *A*, the new point is named *A'*. *A'* is read "*A* prime."

A (1, 5) ──────▶ *A'* (_____ , _____)

B (3, 5) ──────▶ *B'* (_____ , _____)

C (3, 3) ──────▶ *C'* (_____ , _____)

D (1, 3) ──────▶ *D'* (_____ , _____)

Step 2 Plot and label the new points on the grid. Connect the points to show the transformation.

Talk About It

Answer these questions. Use the sentence starters for support.

1. Points *A, B, C,* and *D* are … of the figure.

2. The transformation you did is an example of a …

3. When you used the rule, you changed the … of the figure.

Your Turn

Work with a partner. Draw a triangle on grid paper and label the coordinates. Then switch papers with your partner. Use the rule in Step 1 to do the transformation on your partner's figure. Talk about your work.

Your Turn

A reflection and a rotation are shown below. Write the new coordinates for the points below. (*F'* is read "F prime." *F"* is read "F double prime.")

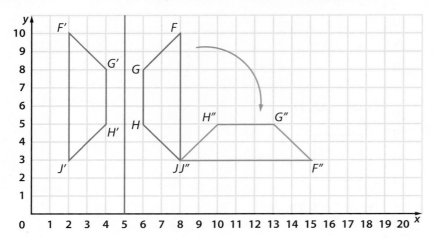

Coordinates after Reflection		Original coordinates		Coordinates after Rotation
(_2_ , _10_) ⟵	F	(_8_ , _10_) ⟶		(_15_ , _3_)
(___ , ___) ⟵	G	(___ , ___) ⟶		(___ , ___)
(___ , ___) ⟵	H	(___ , ___) ⟶		(___ , ___)
(___ , ___) ⟵	J	(___ , ___) ⟶		(___ , ___)

Talk and Write About It

Complete each sentence about transformations.

1 The red trapezoid shows the result of a _____ .

2 The green trapezoid shows the result of a _____ .

3 The vertical line between the red and blue trapezoids is a line

of _____ .

Produce Language

Look back at the terms you rated at the beginning of the lesson. Rate how well you know each term now. Tell a partner what these terms mean in your own words.

Three-Dimensional Figures

Essential Question What vocabulary terms do you need to know and use to talk about three-dimensional figures?

You Will
- Identify three-dimensional figures by their characteristics.
- Identify characteristics of three-dimensional figures.
- Use correct vocabulary when talking about three-dimensional figures.

Talk About It

Look at the list of terms below. Place terms you **know, want** to know more about, and those you have **learned** in class into the chart.

three-dimensional figure	cylinder	prism
face	edge	pyramid
base	parallel faces	rectangular prism
cone	square pyramid	vertex/vertices
cube	triangular prism	triangular pyramid

Know	Want	Learned

Your Turn

Work with a partner and compare your charts. Talk about the terms you wrote in the Know column. You may want to make notes about questions to ask during class discussion.

Vocabulary in Context Picture It!

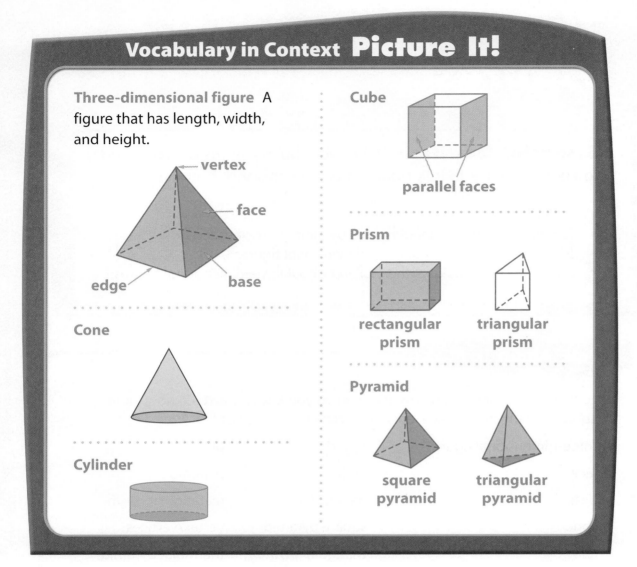

Three-dimensional figure A figure that has length, width, and height.

vertex

face

edge   base

Cone

Cylinder

Cube

parallel faces

Prism

rectangular prism   triangular prism

Pyramid

square pyramid   triangular pyramid

Talk About It

Work with a partner. Match each figure with its name and write the letter next to it. Practice saying each word.

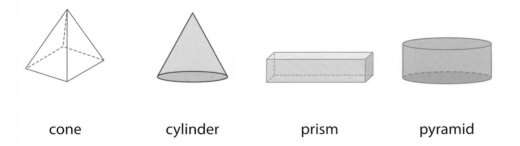

cone   cylinder   prism   pyramid

Your Turn

Work in pairs. Use index cards to make a vocabulary card for each term. Include drawings where you can. Keep the cards for use in future math classes.

Use clay and craft sticks to make three-dimensional figures of a triangular pyramid and a triangular prism.

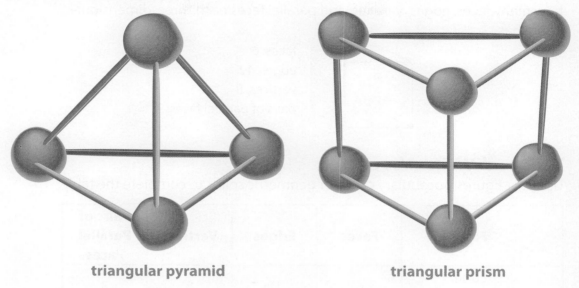

triangular pyramid   triangular prism

Talk About It

Use the figures you built to complete each sentence.

1. The sticks used to build the figures make the … of the figure.

2. The clay pieces used to build the figures make the … of the figure.

3. The shape at each end of the prism you built is its …

Your Turn

Use clay and craft sticks to make three-dimensional figures of a square pyramid and a rectangular prism.

Think, Talk, and Write

Your Turn

Use the figures you built, your vocabulary, and the geometric solids to find how many faces, edges, vertices, and parallel faces each three-dimensional figure has.

Cube: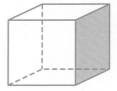
faces: 6
edges: 12
vertices: 8
pairs of parallel faces: 3

Talk and Write About It

Use your figures, vocabulary cards, or geometric solids to complete the table.

	Figure	Faces	Edges	Vertices	Pairs of Parallel Faces
	cube	6	12	8	3
1	square pyramid				
2	rectangular prism				
3	triangular pyramid				
4	triangular prism				

Produce Language

Work in small groups. Explain, and then write, how you might use clay and craft sticks to make a cone and a cylinder.

Hint: Can you make a circle with the clay?

Customary Units of Measurement

Essential Question What terms do you use to describe different measurement units in the customary system?

You Will
- Recognize what various units are used to measure.
- Identify the appropriate unit of measurement to use.
- Use appropriate terms when talking about units of measurement in the customary system of measurement used in the United States.

Talk About It

Follow along as your teacher describes the properties of things that can be measured in the table. For each category, list different units of measurement used in the customary system of measurement used in the United States.

Length	Weight	Liquid Capacity		Time

Your Turn

Work in small groups. Compare your lists and add units to your list. Make a vocabulary card for each unit you listed.

Vocabulary in Context **Picture It!**

Customary system of measurement The system of measurement used in the United States

Length How long an object is

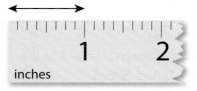

inches

1 **inch** (in.)

1 **foot** (ft) = 12 in.
1 **yard** (yd) = 36 in.
1 **mile** (mi) = 5,280 feet

Time

second (sec)	**week** (wk)
minute (min)	**month** (mo)
hour (hr)	**year** (yr)
day (d)	**decade** (dec)

Weight The number that represents how heavy an object is

5 quarters weigh 1 **ounce** (oz)
1 **pound** (lb) = 16 oz
1 **ton** (T) = 2000 lb

Liquid capacity The amount of liquid that a container can hold

1 **cup** (c) = 8 **fluid ounces** (fl oz)
1 **pint** (pt) = 2 cups
1 **quart** (qt) = 2 pints
1 **gallon** (gal) = 4 quarts

Talk About It

Work with a partner. Complete the sentences.

1. I want to know how heavy something is. I need to find its …

2. I want to know how long my pencil is. I need to find its …

3. I want to know how much water the glass can hold. I need to find its …

Your Turn

Work with a partner. Show your partner the unit on a vocabulary card. He or she must name the property of measurement.

See: | gallon (gal) | Say: liquid capacity

Fill in the table as your class puts the vocabulary cards in the correct places.

Length	Weight	Liquid Capacity	Time	

Talk About It

Work with a partner. Match each unit of measurement with the tool you would use.

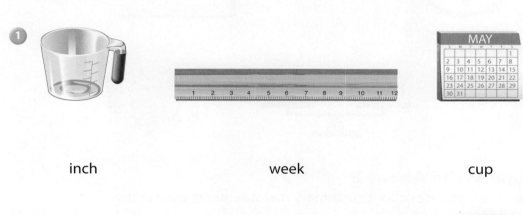

inch   week   cup

yard   pound   hour

Your Turn

Work with a partner. Sort your own vocabulary cards in the same way as the table on the board. For each property, put the units in order from least to greatest. Talk about how you decided the correct order.

Your Turn

To measure in the customary system of measurement, you might use some of these tools.

MAY

Talk and Write About It

Complete the sentences about customary measurements used in the United States.

1. To find your height you could use a ruler marked in _____.

2. When you buy milk in the store, you buy a _____.

3. A calendar shows that there are 7 _____ in 1 _____.

4. To find out what _____ it is, you can look at a clock.

5. You get on a scale to measure your weight in _____.

6. The distance between 2 towns is measured in _____.

Produce Language

Write about how you have used the customary measurement system.

Metric Units of Measurement

Essential Question What terms do you use to describe different measurement units in the metric system?

You Will
- Understand what things can be measured.
- Identify metric units of measure for each property.
- Use appropriate vocabulary when talking about metric units of measure.

Talk About It

Look at the table below. Follow along as your teacher describes the properties of things that can be measured in the table. Next, use the table to help you think of the metric units you can use to measure each property. Put terms in as many places as you can.

Measurement Properties and Units

Length	Mass	Liquid Capacity

Your Turn

Create vocabulary cards for the terms you put in the table. Write the name of the measurement unit on one side of the card and the property it measures on the other side. Include the abbreviation for each unit, if you know it.

Metric system of measurement
The system of measurement based on counting by tens

Length How long an object is

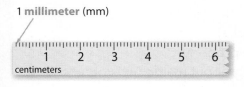

1 **centimeter** (cm)
1 **meter** (m) = 100 cm
1 **kilometer** (km) = 1,000 meters

Mass The amount of matter in an object

1 gram

1 **gram** (g)
1 **kilogram** (kg) = 1,000 grams

Liquid capacity The amount of liquid that a container can hold

1 **milliliter** (ml or mL)
1 **liter** (l or L) = 1,000 mL
1 **kiloliter** (kl or kL) = 1,000 liters

Talk About It

Work with a partner. Complete each sentence.

1. The mass of a watermelon is usually measured in …

2. If you find how many centimeters long a pencil is then you are measuring its …

3. The amount of liquid that a bottle can hold is called its …

Your Turn

Think of the tools you could use to measure different real-life objects. Illustrate each tool and label what it measures. Share your ideas with a partner.

Use the vocabulary cards you made and the table your teacher displayed at the beginning of the lesson. Take turns placing your cards in the appropriate column. When it is your turn, read the unit and its abbreviation from your card. Choose the column where the card belongs. Then, tape the card in that column of the table.

Measurement Properties and Units

Length	Mass	Liquid Capacity

Talk About It

Work with a partner. Match each picture to the unit that best represents it.

1

2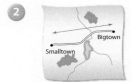

3

4

5

6

a. milliliter

b. kilogram

c. liter

d. kilometers

e. meter

f. centimeter

Your Turn

Sort your vocabulary cards into the different properties. Arrange the units in each property in order from least to greatest.

Your Turn

Look at the pictures. Write the property that is measured in each picture. Then write the best unit of measurement for the picture.

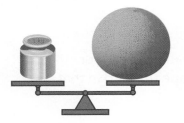

The pan balance measures mass.

The unit of measurement is grams.

Property: _____

Unit of measurement: _____

Property: _____

Unit of measurement: _____

Talk and Write About It

Complete the sentences.

1. A metric unit that you can use to measure your height is

   _____ .

2. A metric unit you can use to the mass of a dog is

   _____ .

3. A metric unit you can use to measure the amount of milk in a bottle is

   _____ .

4. The metric unit of length that measures the distance between two

   cities is _____ .

Produce Language

Write about what you have learned about measurement units in the metric system of measurement.

Area and Perimeter

Essential Question How do you use pictures, numbers, and terms to discuss area and perimeter?

You Will
- Find the area of different shapes.
- Find the perimeter of different shapes.
- Use and understand key terms related to area and perimeter.

Talk About It

Think about area and perimeter. In the first column, write things that you know. In the second column, write things that you want to know.

What I Know	What I Want to Know	What I Learned

Your Turn

Tell a partner what you know and want to know about area and perimeter. Use the sentence starters if you need them.

I know …

I want to know …

Vocabulary in Context **Picture It!**

Perimeter (P) the distance around a figure

Area (A) the number of square units needed to cover a shape

Inch a unit used to measure length and perimeter

1 inch

Square inch a unit used to measure area

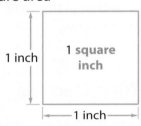

1 inch

1 square inch

1 inch

Dimensions

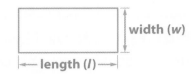

width (*w*)

length (*l*)

Formula an equation that uses variables to state a rule

Perimeter of a rectangle formula

$$P = (2 \times l) + (2 \times w)$$

Area of a rectangle formula

$$A = l \times w$$

Talk About It

Talk with a partner to complete the sentences.

1. The equation $A = l \times w$ is an example of a …

2. … is the number of square units needed to cover a shape.

3. *P* is the symbol for the distance around a figure, or its …

Your Turn

Think of how you would describe the vocabulary terms to someone who does not know them. Write and draw to show what these terms mean to you.

Step 1 Cut out the unit tiles from page 103. Put 8 of them together to make a rectangle like the one below.

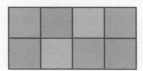

Step 2 Find the perimeter (*P*) of the rectangle. Count the number of units on each side to find the distance around the rectangle or use the formula below.

$P = (2 \times l) + (2 \times w)$

$P = (2 \times \underline{\hspace{1cm}}) + (2 \times \underline{\hspace{1cm}})$

$P = \underline{\hspace{1cm}}$ units

Step 3 Find the number of square inches needed to cover the rectangle, or the area (*A*) of the rectangle. You can count each tile, or you can use the formula below.

$A = l \times w$

$A = \underline{\hspace{1cm}} \times \underline{\hspace{1cm}}$

$A = \underline{\hspace{1cm}}$ square units

Talk About It
Complete the sentences.

1. When you find how many square units make up a figure, you are finding the ... of a figure.

2. You ... the distance around a figure to find its perimeter.

Your Turn
Draw a triangle. Find the perimeter of the triangle. Share your answer with a partner.

Your Turn

Make a plan for a school bookstore. Use between 10 and 16 1-inch unit tiles from page 103. Arrange the tiles on the grid below. Each tile must touch at least one side of another tile. Find the perimeter of your bookstore. Find the area.

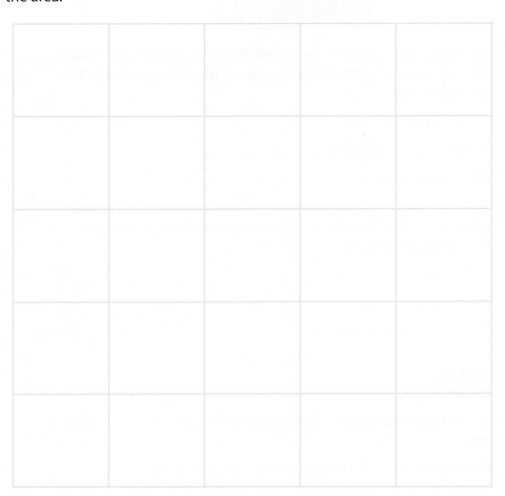

Talk and Write About It

1. The shape of the bookstore is a ...

2. I used 1-inch ... to measure the area.

3. I used a ruler to find the ... of each side so I could calculate the ..., or distance around the bookstore.

Produce Language

Write about what you learned in the chart from the beginning of the lesson. Use sentence starters from throughout the lesson for support.

Volume and Surface Area

Essential Question What vocabulary terms do you need to know to talk about the formulas for finding volume and surface area of rectangular prisms?

You Will
- Talk about the formulas used for finding the volume and surface area of rectangular prisms.
- Understand what the variables in formulas stand for.
- Use vocabulary terms when talking about formulas.

Talk About It

Look at the list of terms below. Place terms you **know, want** to know more about, and those you have **learned** in class into the chart.

rectangular prism	cube	surface area
length (*l*)	side (*s*)	square foot
width (*w*)	base (*B*)	cubic foot
height (*h*)	volume	formula

Know	Want	Learned

Your Turn
Work in small groups. Explain what you are going to learn. Use the sentence starter for support.

I will learn about …

Vocabulary in Context **Picture It!**

Rectangular prism   **Cube**

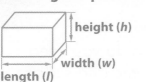

height (*h*)

width (*w*)

length (*l*)

side (*s*)

Base (*B*) The area of the base of a three-dimensional figure.

Base (*B*)

Volume The number of cubic units that will fit inside of a three-dimensional figure.

Surface area The sum of the areas of all the faces of a prism.

Square foot A unit used to measure area.

Cubic foot A unit used to measure volume.

Formula An equation that uses variables to state a rule.

Talk About It

Work in small groups. One student reads the sentence starter. Then each student tries to complete that sentence on his or her own. Discuss your answers as a group.

1. A … is an equation that uses variables to state a rule.

2. If you want to know how many cubic units will fit in a three-dimensional figure, you need to find its …

3. If you want to know the total area of all the faces of a rectangular prism, you need to find its …

Your Turn

Work in small groups. Talk about each vocabulary term. Share examples and practice saying each word.

Below are some formulas for finding volume and surface area.

Volume formulas

rectangular prism: $V = lwh$ or $V = Bh$

cube: $V = s^3$

Surface area formulas

rectangular prism: $SA = 2(lw) + 2(hw) + 2(lh)$

cube: $SA = 6s^2$

Remember, sometimes the multiplication sign is not shown because it could be confused with a variable. *lwh* means *l* times *w* times *h*.

What the variables mean:

V: volume

SA: surface area

h: height

l: length

w: width

B: area of the base of a three-dimensional figure

s: length of a side of a square face of a cube

Talk About It

Work with a partner. Name the formula that is described.

1. This formula says to multiply the length (*l*) times the width (*w*). Then multiply that product by the height (*h*).

2. This formula says to multiply the length of a side (*s*) times itself. Then multiply that product by 6.

3. This formula says to find twice the product of the length (*l*) and width (*w*), plus twice the product of the height (*h*) and width (*w*), plus twice the product of the length (*l*) and height (*h*).

4. This formula says to multiply the length of a side (*s*) by itself and then multiply that product by the length of the side again.

Your Turn

Write each formula on a separate index card. Write what the formula is used to find on the card. Also be sure to write what the variables used in the formula represent.

Your Turn

The work of four students is shown below. Can you figure out what each of them calculated? Talk it over with your partner. Refer to the formulas for help.

Andre

$8 \times 8 = 64$
$6 \times 64 = 384$

384 square feet

Shinji

$2(8 \times 4) + 2(5 \times 4) + 2(8 \times 5)$
$\qquad = 64 + 40 + 80 = 184$

184 square feet

Felicia

$4 \times 8 \times 6 = 192$

192 cubic feet

Simona

$7 \times 7 \times 7 = 49 \times 7 = 343$

343 cubic feet

Volume formulas   rectangular prism: $V = lwh$ or $V = Bh$
cube: $V = s^3$

Surface area formulas   rectangular prism: $SA = 2(lw) + 2(hw) + 2(lh)$
cube: $SA = 6s^2$

Talk and Write About It

Complete the sentences.

1. Andre figured out the _____ of a _____.

2. Shinji figured out the _____ of a _____.

3. Felicia figured out the _____ of a _____.

4. Simona figured out the _____ of a _____.

Produce Language

Work in small groups. Look back at the chart you began on page 81. In the third column, write what you have learned. Include sentences that tell what each formula is used to find and what the variables in the formula represent.

Graphic Representations

Essential Question What vocabulary terms do you need to know and use to talk about graphic representations?

You Will
- Identify different kinds of graphs and charts.
- Describe the information shown in different displays.
- Understand and use key terms relating to different graphs and charts.

Talk About It

Rate these mathematical terms according to the following scale:

I have never heard of this term before.

I have heard this term before, but I do not know how to use it in mathematics.

I understand the meaning of this term and know how to use it in mathematics.

_____ Circle Graph   _____ Data

_____ Line Plot   _____ Histogram

_____ Stem-and-Leaf Plot   _____ Venn Diagram

_____ Line Graph

Your Turn
Explain what you think you are going to learn. Use the sentence starter for support.

I will learn about …

Vocabulary in Context Picture It!

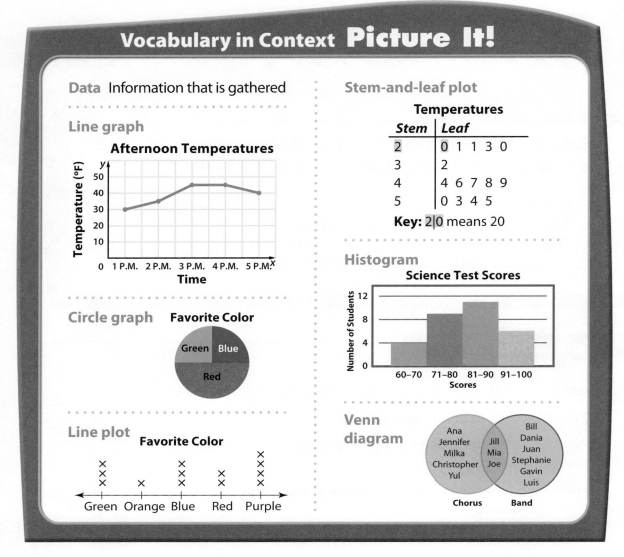

Data Information that is gathered

Line graph

Afternoon Temperatures

Circle graph Favorite Color

Green Blue

Red

Line plot Favorite Color

Green Orange Blue Red Purple

Stem-and-leaf plot

Temperatures

Stem	Leaf
2	0 1 1 3 0
3	2
4	4 6 7 8 9
5	0 3 4 5

Key: 2|0 means 20

Histogram

Science Test Scores

Venn diagram

Ana Jennifer Milka Christopher Yul / Jill Mia Joe / Bill Dania Juan Stephanie Gavin Luis

Chorus   Band

Talk About It

Talk with a partner to complete the sentences.

1. A … is a graph that uses bars that touch to show data.

2. A … shows a circle divided into sections.

Your Turn

Describe what each display looks like. Share your ideas with a partner.

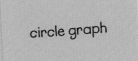

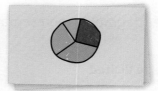

Work with a partner to play a vocabulary matching game. One person draws each of these on a separate card: line graph, circle graph, line plot, Venn diagram, stem-and-leaf plot, histogram. The partner writes each term on a separate card.

Step 1 Sort the cards. Make a pile for terms and another pile for pictures.

Step 2 One partner takes the picture pile and the other takes the term pile.

Step 3 One partner shows a picture card. The other partner tries to find the matching term card.

To make a match, the partner must tell about the vocabulary term and a good way to remember it.

Step 4 Repeat until all cards have been matched.

Step 5 Switch cards and play again.

Talk About It

Answer these questions using the sentence starters for support if you need it.

1 How can you remember what a line graph is? I remember that a line graph shows …

2 What display do you think of when you think of a plant with a single stem and many leaves? I think of a …

Your Turn

Think of a few sentences that describe how data is presented on a circle graph and on a histogram. Draw your ideas as you share them with a partner.

Think, Talk, and Write

Your Turn

Work in pairs. Name each graphic representation.

States We've Visited

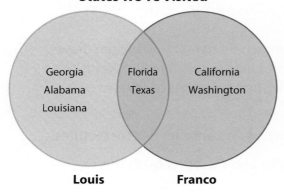

Louis   Franco

_____

Temperature Lows in Columbus

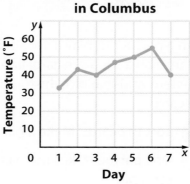

_____

Health Test Scores

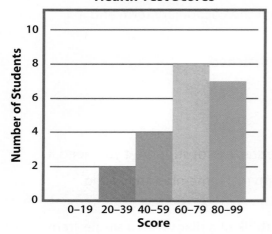

_____

Computers Sold Each Month

4	0 1 1 3 0
5	2
6	4 6 8 9
7	0 3

Key: 4|0 means 40

_____

Talk and Write About It

Complete each sentence about the graphs.

1. The line graph shows _____ about the temperatures in Columbus.

2. The _____ explains how the information is shown on the stem-and-leaf plot.

3. The _____ shows data about test scores.

4. The _____ shows the cities visited by two boys.

Produce Language

Work with a partner to write a few sentences describing each graph.

Mean, Median, Mode, and Range

Essential Question How do you explain mean, median, mode, and range for the set of data shown in a graph?

You Will
- Find and describe sets of data using the ideas of mean, median, mode, and range.
- Use correct vocabulary when describing and interpreting sets of data.

Talk About It

Look at the list of terms below. Place terms you **know, want** to know more about, and those you have **learned** in class into

data   graph

mean   median

mode   range

outlier

Know	Want	Learned

Your Turn
Describe the graph. What do you want to learn?

Vocabulary in Context **Picture It!**

Data Information that is gathered

Graph A diagram used to show a set of data

Mean The average of a set of data

Data: 8, 3, 4, 8, 7

$$\frac{8 + 3 + 4 + 8 + 7}{5} = ⑥ \leftarrow \text{mean}$$

Median The middle number in a set of data

Data: 3, 4, ⑦ 8, 8

⎿————— median

Mode The number that appears most often in a set of data

Data: 3, 4, 7, ⑧, ⑧ ⟵ mode

Range The difference between the greatest and least numbers in a set of data

Data: 3, 4, 7, 8, 8

$$8 - 3 = ⑤ \leftarrow \text{range}$$

Outlier A number that is far away from other numbers in a set of data

Data: 3, 4, 7, 8, ㉒ ⟵ outlier

Talk About It

Look at these tests scores. Complete each sentence.

1. 70 appears most often, so 70 is the …

2. The middle score is 80, so 80 is the …

3. Jeff added all his scores and divided by 5 to get 82, so 82 is the …

4. Jeff subtracted the least number from the greatest number and got 30, so 30 is the …

5. A score of 35 on Jeff's next test would be far away from the other scores, so 35 would be an …

> **Jeff's Math Test Scores**
> 70 70 80 90 100

Your Turn

Talk to your partner about what these terms mean to you.

How Many Books We Read in May

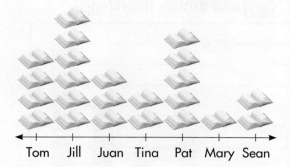

Tom   Jill   Juan   Tina   Pat   Mary   Sean

Work with a partner to analyze the set of data in the graph. Write the correct number on each answer blank.

• The data set for this graph is 4, 6, 3, 2, _____, _____, _____.

• The difference between the greatest and least number of books read

  is _____.

• The middle number for the number of books read is _____.

• The average number of books read is _____.

• The number of books that was read the most is _____.

Talk About It

Use the graph and your answers above. Talk with a partner to complete each sentence with the terms *mean, median, mode,* or *range*. Discuss why you chose each term.

1 5 is the …

2 3 is the …

3 3.3 is the …

4 2 is the …

Your Turn

Explain to a partner how to find the mean, median, mode, and range of a data set.

Your Turn

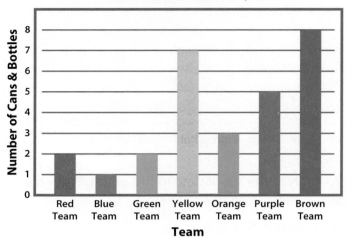

Cans and Bottles Recycled

Use the data in the graph above. Match each term with its value.

1. mean _____   **a.** 2
2. median _____   **b.** 3
3. mode _____   **c.** 4
4. range _____   **d.** 7

Talk and Write About It

Complete these sentences.

1. The middle number in a set of data is called the _____.

2. When you add up all of the numbers in a set of data and divide by the number of numbers, you get the _____.

3. The difference between the greatest and least numbers in a set of data is the _____.

4. The number that appears the most often is called the _____.

5. There are no numbers in this set of data far away from the other numbers, so this set of data does not have an _____.

Produce Language

Use the chart you started on page 89 to write about what you learned.

Probability

Essential Question What do you need to need to know and use to discuss probability?

You Will
- Identify the outcomes in a probability experiment.
- Understand what a tree diagram represents.
- Understand and use key terms related to probability.

Talk About It

Rate these mathematical terms according to the following scale:

1. I have never heard of this term before.

2. I have heard this term before, but I do not know how to use it in mathematics.

3. I understand the meaning of this term and know how to use it in mathematics

_____ Probability   _____ Tree Diagram

_____ Outcome   _____ Heads

_____ Possible Outcomes   _____ Tails

_____ Favorable Outcome

Your Turn
Explain what you expect to learn in this lesson. Use the sentence starter to help you.

I am going to learn about …

Vocabulary in Context Picture It!

Outcome A result

. . . .

Possible outcomes The different things that can happen

The possible outcomes of a coin toss are **heads** and **tails.**

. . . .

Favorable outcome The outcome that you want to know more about

. . . .

Probability The likelihood, or chance, that something will happen

Probability of an event $= \dfrac{\text{number of favorable outcomes}}{\text{total number of possible outcomes}}$

The probability of getting heads on a coin toss is $\dfrac{1}{2}$.

. . . .

Tree diagram

First student	Second student	Outcome
Girl	Girl	Girl, Girl
	Boy	Girl, Boy
Boy	Girl	Boy, Girl
	Boy	Boy, Boy

Talk About It

Work with another student to complete the sentences.

1. The chance that an event will happen is called its …

2. A result is also called an …

3. When you toss a coin, the possible outcomes are … and …

Your Turn

Talk to your partner. Describe the terms in this lesson.

Look at the cards that the teacher is holding up. Suppose the teacher puts the cards in a bag. What is the probability that you will pick a red card? Follow the steps and write the numbers on the answer blanks.

Step 1 List the possible outcomes when you draw one card from the bag of three cards? _____, _____, _____

Step 2 Find the total number of possible outcomes. Count the cards. _____

Step 3 Find the number of favorable outcomes. Count the red cards. _____

Step 4 Write the fraction.

$$\frac{\text{number of favorable outcomes}}{\text{total number of possible outcomes}} = \underline{\qquad}$$

This is the probability.

Talk About It

Complete the sentences.

1 The likelihood or chance of an event is called its …

2 Using the cards shown above, the probability of choosing a blue card is …

3 The probability of picking a brown card is …

Your Turn

Describe how to find the probability of picking an orange card.

Your Turn

Two spinners are divided equally into three sections. The tree diagram below shows the possible outcomes of spinning both spinners. Complete the tree diagram.

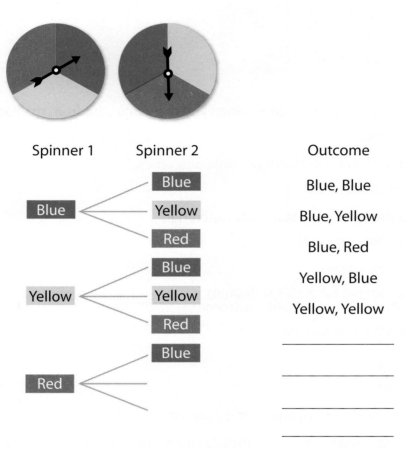

Spinner 1	Spinner 2	Outcome
	Blue	Blue, Blue
Blue	Yellow	Blue, Yellow
	Red	Blue, Red
	Blue	Yellow, Blue
Yellow	Yellow	Yellow, Yellow
	Red	
	Blue	
Red		

Talk and Write About It

Complete the sentences.

1 This diagram is called a _____.

2 The total number of possible outcomes shown in the tree diagram is _____.

3 _____ of the possible outcomes show two cards of the same color.

Produce Language

Write what you have learned about probability. Use the vocabulary and the activities for support.

Equivalent Fraction Strips

✂

1	2	3	4	5	6	7	8	9	10	11	12
2	4	6	8	10	12	14	16	18	20	22	24
3	6	9	12	15	18	21	24	27	30	33	36
4	8	12	16	20	24	28	32	36	40	44	48
5	10	15	20	25	30	35	40	45	50	55	60
6	12	18	24	30	36	42	48	54	60	66	72
7	14	21	28	35	42	49	56	63	70	77	84
8	16	24	32	40	48	56	64	72	80	88	96
9	18	27	36	45	54	63	72	81	90	99	108
10	20	30	40	50	60	70	80	90	100	110	120
11	22	33	44	55	66	77	88	99	110	121	132
12	24	36	48	60	72	84	96	108	120	132	144

Slope Four Corners Activity

Corner 1

Corner 2

Slope Four Corners Activity

Corner 3

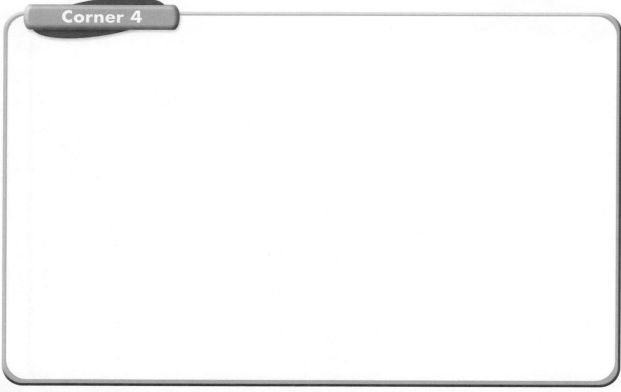

Corner 4

Slope Four Corners Activity

Cut out each graph and glue it in the box that has the matching equation.

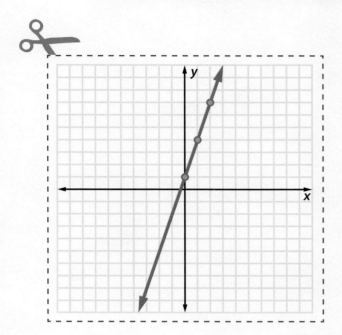

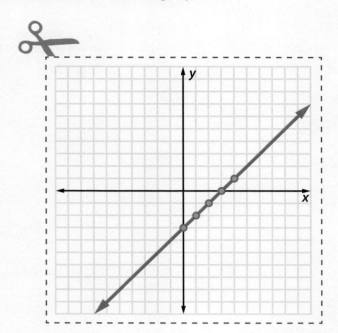

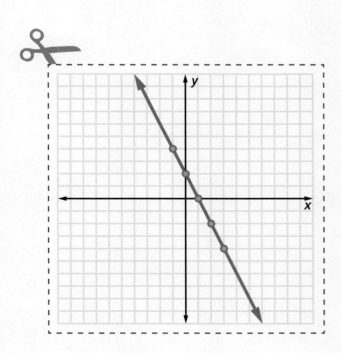

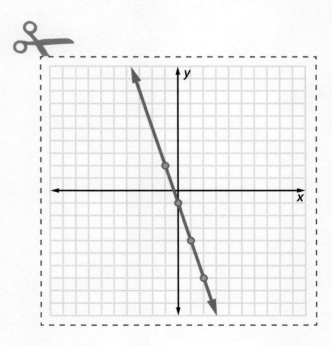

Unit Tiles